This written family the I hope it will help your future relationships.

I love you very much!

Jan

# 12 Best Kept Secrets

## To a Fulfilling Relationship

Dr. Jeff Kane

Parker House Publishing
www.ParkerHouseBooks.com

ISBN: 978-0-9895474-3-7

Disclaimer: The advice offered in this book is not intended to replace the diagnosis or treatment of psychological or relationship problems. If you are experiencing mental health or relationship concerns, it is recommended that you hire a qualified, licensed mental health care professional.

# What People Are Saying...

## Relationship Coaching Services via Skype/Telephone

*"I was referred to Dr. Kane by a trusted colleague and friend of mine 2 years ago. I was unsure if telephone and Skype consultations would have the impact I desired because the experience was new to my wife and I. After our first meeting, we were hooked! The connection was seamless and I we were able to meet with him right from the comfort of my home in the evening. Dr. Kane is a true professional in every sense of the word. He helped us alleviate problems that had been in our lives for over a decade. We loved his humor and his genuineness. The relief we felt was enormous and he gave us the tools to let go of a bunch of 'stuff' that had harmed our relationship for too long! To this day, my wife and I continue to meet with the 'Doc' for check-ups on a monthly basis. Several of my friends and colleagues have found success working with him as well. Dr. Kane is the best!"*

~ Robert & Samantha, San Francisco, CA

*"We have seen several counselors over the 20 years of our marriage with little success. After being referred by a close friend, my husband and I were immediately impressed with his patience, kindness and understanding. Most of the change we received in the past was short-lived. With Dr. Kane's gentle guidance, he helped us uncover and resolve underlying*

*emotions and behaviors that were suffocating our relationship for years. Each week he gave us homework and practical guidance that changed our relationship. We are forever grateful to Dr. Kane and are thankful to work with him. He is a true professional in every sense of the word."*

~ Laura & Michael, Sydney, Australia


*"My husband and I had the pleasure of meeting with Dr. Kane over the past few months. Since we live in the UK, the only way we could meet with Dr. Kane was through Skype. Our nightly meetings were a breath of fresh air for our relationship. Dr. Kane offered practical and real life solutions that improved our relationship. We both loved Dr. Kane's humor and warm disposition. After the first consultation, we knew that we had found the right person to help us get to a better place. Dr. Kane is a true relationship expert and saved our marriage. We plan on keeping in touch with him as we continue to enjoy our happy, healthy relationship. We appreciate Dr. Kane. He is the best!"*

~ Charles & Jacqueline, London, England


## Coaching Program

*"My wife and I had the pleasure of taking part in Dr. Kane's 'Relationship Secrets Program' – a program that brings the book you are reading to life. We were referred by*

*another couple that worked with Dr. Kane in his office and we were excited to be able to experience his expertise from 3500 miles away. We have been 'in and out' of couple's therapy without success. Dr. Kane's program "hit the nail on the head" of our problems and really made us look at our relationship in a different way. He really understands the 'real-life' problems relationships experience. I believe that our marriage would have ended if we never met Dr. Kane. We are grateful for the healing and the 'spark' that has been created thanks to his program. Thanks Doc!"*

~Bonnie & Scott, Alberta, Canada


**In Person**


*"We have seen several counselors over the 20 years of our marriage with little success. After being referred by a close friend, my husband and I were immediately impressed with his patience, kindness and understanding. Most of the change we received in the past was short-lived. With Dr. Kane's gentle guidance, he helped us uncover and resolve underlying emotions and behaviors that were suffocating our relationship for years. Each week he gave us homework and practical guidance that changed our relationship. We are forever grateful to Dr. Kane and are thankful to work with him. He is a true processional in every sense of the word."*

~ Lisa and Mark, Weston. Florida

"We were referred to Dr. Kane from a good friend. For years we had been in and out of therapy. Unfortunately, the changes that occurred in therapy never lasted. After feeling quite disillusioned about therapy and our marriage, we decided to meet with Dr. Kane. He was a breath of fresh air. He is so humble and easy to talk with. Both my husband and I felt that he was neutral and listened objectively to both of our perspectives. Dr. Kane offered unique and creative ways to introduce change into our relationship that had been stuck in the same place for so many years. We even had a few laughs in therapy thanks to Dr. Kane's great sense of humor. To this day, I refer my friends, family & associates to Dr. Kane. He is an expert in working with couples and a true professional. We have been blessed to have him in our life and know he's always there if we need him. Thanks, Doc!"

~ Rachael & Martin, Parkland, Florida

## Dedication

I would like to thank my wife, Sherry, for her love and support. You have always been by my side and a source of strength in my life. Sherry, you are the love of my life, my best friend and an incredible mother to our sons. Many of the "secrets" shared in this book have been the key to the longevity of our marriage of nearly 20 years.

I also dedicate this book to my amazing boys. Jordan and Jeremy, you keep me young and help me relive the incredible memories of my childhood. The playfulness and strength that both of you display are qualities that will serve you well as you move forward in life. Jordan and Jeremy I love you with all of my heart.

# Foreword

When you are fulfilled in a relationship you feel alive, excited and wanting more. What's better than waking up to a person who you know is invested emotionally, psychologically and spiritually in your relationship? Isn't it great to feel passionate about the person you are spending your life with?

Everyone wants the kind of relationship they imagine in their mind's eye, but the reality is, the dream doesn't always live up to the expectation. The person you thought was with you in good times and bad is suddenly distant and you wonder how such strong feelings could change so dramatically. How can such intense passion fade in a relatively short span of time and can it be recaptured once it seems to have faded away? How long is the road to recovery?

If you have ever experienced that or asked yourself these kinds of questions you are in the right place. If you are looking for answers this can be the opportunity to start finding them. Don't we all want answers to why things go wrong? It's also helpful to find some solutions as well. While exploring the "12 Best Kept Secrets to a Fulfilling Relationship," you will have the opportunity to find some solutions. The solutions can make a difference in your life if you invest your time and practice patience in the process of changing your relationship. The mere act of reading these secrets will only open the door to creating change very slightly. After that, it's up to you to walk in, explore, check things out, and see how your life and relationship can change if you do the work that's needed.

Much of the change will only occur if you are willing to go "all in." You will have an opportunity to take a peek into some new ways of seeing relationships. This is a good start. Where you go from here is up to you. So, try to see the information as a general roadmap. It's totally up to you if you go on the journey or just stay in your car and read the map. If you ever explored the mountains, you know that it is way more fun grabbing your backpack, putting on your hiking shoes and tackling the mountain than just staring at boring maps. Those who take the adventure are rewarded. Those who stay on the sidelines will just dream of how life "could have been." So, which path are you planning to take?

I invite you to come explore the "12 Best Kept Secrets of a Fulfilling Relationship." The "secrets" will allow you to navigate different parts of your relationship. I encourage you to answer the questions at the end of each section and participate in the exercises. Have fun exploring the "secrets" and allow your thoughts to venture into new, unchartered waters. The only way change happens is if you leave your comfort zone and challenge yourself to think differently.

# Table of Contents

# SECRET #1

## Establish an Atmosphere of Emotional Support

Showing emotional support is an important ingredient in creating a strong foundation in a relationship. When you show emotional support you are able to accept your partner's differences without insisting that he or she meet your needs in the precise way that you want them met. To achieve an atmosphere of emotional support, one must re-orient his or her perspective. Emotional awareness is greatly connected to emotional support. Becoming emotionally aware of your needs will better help your partner fulfill your needs. All too often, there is a guessing game that occurs where the couple is trying to figure out the emotional needs of his or her significant other. This process can become rather tiring and keep you stuck.

> *Remember, you and your partner are in the relationship together so try not to make yourself the facilitator for the entire relationship.*

One way of understanding emotional support is to compare it to emotional demands. Emotional support for each other is critical. This means giving your partner a feeling of being backed and supported; you're behind him or her no matter what. This does not necessarily mean agreeing with one another all the time. Realistically, no two people will agree on all occasions. What it does mean is you treat your partner in a way that says, "I love you and trust you, and I'm with you through anything."

Emotional demands can damage the relationship. Each of these is an emotional demand, and has potential for damaging the relationship:

- Insisting that your partner spend all of his or her time with you

- Insisting that they give up their friends or that you both hang around only your friends

- Insisting that you give approval of the clothes they wear, making sure you make all the decisions about how you spend your time together and where you go when you go out

- Making them feel guilty when they spend time with their families

- Making sure you win all the arguments

- Always insisting that your feelings are the most important

Emotional support involves accepting how your partner is different from you and not insisting that they meet your needs in the precise way you want them met. An example might be when you want your partner to show love for you by spending free time with you, sharing and being open, paying attention to your concerns and needs. Of course these are important activities, but your partner may often show his or her love by sharing home responsibilities, bringing you gifts occasionally, discussing the day's events or books and movies you've shared.

Explore with your partner how he or she shows love for you. It's great to "paint a picture" for one another and tell each other what you like. Make it easier on one another so you can create a stronger love. Remember, too, that the words, "I love you. I like being in a relationship with you. You're important to me," are not demands and need to be said occasionally in any relationship.

Life is often challenging and it is difficult to always meet your partner's emotional needs. Understanding your own emotional needs is a great starting point. If you are unsure of your emotions and how you are feeling, how can you begin to manage the emotionality of a relationship?  Be honest with your partner about how you are feeling so he or she can understand your position. If you completely ignore your emotional needs, the relationship will suffer. And if you do not openly share your emotions your partner will be left to "guess" how to respond to your behavior. Try to keep "guessing" out of the equation and instead clarify how you feel on a regular basis. This will enhance your relationship and create a closer emotional bond.

As part of our **Relationship Coaching Program** at Relationships Unscripted, we explore the emotional connection that couples share. Your relationship will be enhanced when unspoken thoughts are shared.  If you find that you are lacking an emotional connection to your partner there are usually underlying issues that need to be addressed. By ignoring the disconnection your relationship will usually deteriorate over time.

There are many reasons why a couple is emotionally distant from one another. Frequently it's a result of problems or issues that have been swept under the rug. Creating an illusion that problems do not exist keeps the problems around longer, and your emotions will begin to change. You may also find that how you feel about your partner will change. Over time, it will become increasingly difficult to bridge the gap. Staying emotionally connected is something that has to occur on a weekly basis. Waiting until the emotional distance has been created and then attempting to "save" the relationship is a much longer road to travel.

When I meet with couples over the Internet or in my office, I remind them that without emotions there is "no relationship." Emotions are the foundation of a vibrant, growing relationship. Sometimes it may appear that the emotions have left the relationship or that one or both partners seemingly no longer have emotions when it comes to the relationship. Of course, this isn't the case because as humans, we are always experiencing some kind of emotion.

It may seem like the emotional connection has been completely lost; in fact, it's just that the emotions are hidden because one partner is feeling hurt, angry, betrayed or resentful. So, as a means of protection, he or she begins to behave in a non-emotional way. Just because emotions are not shared does not mean they do not exist. In order for emotions to be share, however, a couple must create a safe and nurturing environment.

Each partner has to feel comfortable opening up without concern that he or she is going to be scrutinized, demeaned or made to feel incompetent. How would you like to share your emotions with someone who looks at you as if you are "silly" or "ridiculous"? Probably not. Why would you talk openly with someone if you think it will be a waste of time?

Sharing your emotions makes you vulnerable. Being vulnerable can be a valuable experience as long as it is with someone who will embrace your emotionality. Why share and be open if your partner looks at you without compassion? Holding your loved one's hand or looking in his or her eyes shows that you care. How did you share your emotions when you first started dating? How long has it been since you expressed your emotions in your relationship and felt supported? Recalling positive memories of past behavior can sometimes be a great start. Recall what you used to do that worked. Recapturing emotions is not an easy process and takes time as well as patience. If you are invested in a relationship your behavior has to show your dedication on an emotional level. Without emotions you have no relationship.

Some questions you may want to consider:

- In what areas does your partner need emotional support? What is your role in providing this support?

- Has the emotional support you have for your partner changed over time? If so, how has the emotional needs of the relationship changed?

- Are you able to meet the emotional needs of your relationship?

Be honest with each other as you explore these areas. Without honesty the experience of sharing will result in little change and a continued feeling of being stuck. Change is not easy and takes two willing and motivated people who want to do whatever is necessary to have a fulfilling relationship.

Emotional support is a key ingredient for a good relationship and when both people feel they are emotionally supported, the relationship will grow in a way that reflects its strong foundation. Everything is easier when sincere, consistent emotional support is in place.

One of the greatest needs for any person is to feel they are accepted and not judged. Emotional support provides that sense of security and creates a space within the relationship where new things can be tested and tried without fear of withdrawal from the other person.

As the relationship matures, this will become increasingly important, as no relationship is able to flourish without new things being introduced. Some of these will be voluntary and some will be a result of life happening but a couple who knows the strong bonds of emotional support will be able to withstand life's ups and downs better together. What can you do today to begin to increase your emotional support of your partner?

**Relationship Exercise:**

Sit down with your partner to create an "emotional list" that includes all the emotional needs that he or she desires to have met in the relationship. Do the same for yourself. What did you learn from reviewing your lists? Are they similar or different? How?

# SECRET #2

## Establish a Pattern of Apologizing

An integral part of a strong relationship is being able to establish a pattern of apologizing if you make a mistake or hurt your partner's feelings. Saying "I'm sorry" may be hard in the moment, but it goes a long way towards healing a rift in a relationship. Your partner will trust you more if he or she knows that you will take responsibility for your words and actions.

9

When I work with couples, I find that one of the greatest obstacles during the process of apologizing is for them to admit their errors. Perfection is an unrealistic goal for any relationship. Imperfect people create imperfect relationships. Everyone has flaws and apologizing brings a greater appreciation to your significant other and lets them know that you care about his or her feelings. It's quite important that your apologies are heartfelt and real. There is nothing worse than apologizing to your partner and he or she realizes that you were faking it. Pretending to care is different than genuine caring. The act of apologizing shows the depth of your love and your emotional connection to your loved one.

Often, we tend to view apologies as a sign of weak character in a relationship. But in fact, they require great strength as well as a willingness to be vulnerable. When you apologize you are showing humility and inviting your relationship to grow.

The process of learning and growing in a relationship never truly ends. A genuine apology offered and accepted is one of the most profound interactions of civilized people. It has the power to restore damaged relationships, be they on a small scale between two people, such as intimates, or on a grand scale between groups of people or even nations. If done correctly, an apology can heal humiliation and generate forgiveness.

Yet, even though it's such a powerful social skill, we give precious little thought to teaching our children how to apologize. Most of us never learned very well ourselves. The emotional environment that you were exposed to as a child sets the tone for how you understand apologizing. Did you see your parents or adults around you openly apologize to one another? How often did you hear an adult say, "I am sorry for hurting your feelings." Of course, despite the limitations that your environment may have created for you as a child, there is absolutely nothing preventing you from altering this pattern as an adult. It just requires some self-awareness and reminding yourself to show your sincerity when you have hurt your loved one's feelings. As I often tell clients I work with, "You are perfectly imperfect."

Despite its importance, apologizing is antithetical to the ever-pervasive values of winning, success, and perfection. The successful apology in a relationship requires empathy and the security and strength to admit fault, failure, and weakness. Too often, however, we are so busy winning that we can't concede our own mistakes.

I frequently talk with couples about the "botched apology" -- the apology intended but not delivered, or delivered but not accepted, which has serious social consequences. Failed apologies can strain relationships beyond repair or worse, create life-long grudges and bitter vengeance.

If you are not genuine, your apology will make things worse in your relationship. Being genuine about your apology does not mean you "fake it" without the person knowing. To be genuine about an apology, it has to come from a place of deep meaning and significance. If you care about your partner, it would follow that you feel bad when you said or did something to hurt their feelings. Apology is not about right and wrong. It's about showing you care about the other person's feelings.

Sometimes a partner does not apologize because they hold the feeling that they're "right" and you're "wrong." One of the best ways of deteriorating a relationship is to argue about right and wrong. Apologizing is not about right/wrong or good/bad; it's about beginning the process of healing the relationship. Knowing that your significant other cares is the first step in releasing the animosity and allowing the relationship to heal.

The act of apologizing is easy once you leave your ego behind. You may ask yourself, "What is more important, my ego or my relationship? The answer to this question will tell you a lot about you and your relationship. When choosing your ego over your relationship, your ego will always win and your relationship will suffer. Conversely, choosing your relationship over your ego will result in a stronger and more connected relationship.

If you find you have to repress how you feel to benefit your relationship there are probably some underlying concerns that need to be addressed. Does your relationship create space to be able to talk about what may be uncomfortable? If you have found that your openness has not been embraced or well-received in your relationship you may be hesitant to be open about what you are feeling. Your feelings are important and are not necessarily related to your ego. To be happy in a relationship, you have to be yourself, feelings included.

Over the years I've worked with couples who have remained stuck because of their decision to not apologize to their partner. The negative feelings and resentfulness eats away at the fabric of their relationship. The failure to apologize has created destruction in their relationship. Simply stated, grudges can be avoided altogether or simply reconciled with a genuine apology.

No doubt the most compelling and common reason to apologize is over a personal offense. Whether we've ignored, belittled, betrayed, or publicly humiliated someone, the common denominator of any personal offense is that we've diminished or injured that person's self-concept. The self-concept is our belief about us. It's our thoughts and feelings about who we are, how we would like to be, and how we would like to be perceived by others.

If you think of yourself as a competent, highly valued professional and are asked tomorrow by your boss to move into a cramped windowless office, you would likely be personally offended. You might be insulted and feel hurt or humiliated. No matter whether the interpersonal wound is delivered in a professional, family, or social setting, its depth is determined by three factors:

1.  The meaning the event carries to the offended party,

2.  The relationship between the offender and the offended, and

3.  The vulnerability of the offended to take things personally.

Once the personal offense has been made and the blow to the self-concept landed, an apology is demanded or expected. Why bother? Here are four basic motives for apologizing:

1.  To salvage or restore the relationship. Whether you've hurt someone you love or just plain need as your ally in an office situation, an apology may well rekindle the troubled relationship.

2.  You may have purely empathic reasons for apologizing. You regret that you have caused someone to suffer and you apologize to diminish or end their pain.

The last two motives are not so lofty:

3.  Some people apologize simply to escape punishment, such as the criminal who apologizes to his victim in exchange for a lesser plea.

4.  Others apologize simply to relieve themselves of a guilty conscience. They feel so ashamed of what they did, even though it may not have bothered them that much, they then apologize profusely. A long letter explaining why the offender was a half hour late to dinner is an example of this behavior. In so doing, they are trying to maintain some self-respect, because they are nurturing an image of themselves in which the offense, lack of promptness, violates some basic self-concept.

Some questions you may want to consider:

- How can you apologize to your partner in a way that shows you genuinely care?

- What is the goal and what do you hope to accomplish with your apology?

- Are you apologizing because you feel guilty or truly care about your partner's feelings?

- Do you ever fake an apology just to make everything okay?

- If you haven't been "real" in your relationship, have you created the illusion that everything is fine when it's really not?

One last word about apologies; they can be tough when you know you are in the wrong and feel downright impossible to deliver when you feel as if you did nothing wrong. There are going to be times, however, when a contentious situation requires that someone steps up and apologizes first and that person may be you, even if you are the last person who should apologize. Usually one apology will yield another though, so keep that in mind when you feel your partner is the one who should definitely apologize first. If you examine the situation, you'll probably find that somewhere in there, you had some kind of contribution! So go ahead and apologize first for your part in things and watch what happens. You'll be glad you stepped up.

### Relationship Exercise:

Take a personal inventory of your relationship and write down the TOP 10 apologies that you have *never* given to your partner. Begin the healing process by sharing these apologies with your loved one and let him or her know why you did not apologize sooner.

# SECRET #3

## Clarify Your Messages

An important part of communication in a relationship is being able to clearly express your way of seeing the world. Clarifying a message involves a respectful yet direct expression of your wants and needs. Take some time to identify what you really want before talking to your partner. Work on being able to describe your request in clear, observable terms. For example, you might say, "I would like you to hold my hand more often" rather than the vague, "I wish you were more affectionate."

Communication occurs on different levels in a relationship. The verbal part should convey your perspective. One of the greatest challenges in a relationship is being able to express your thoughts clearly and succinctly. The best way to become good at clarifying your message is through practice. Create opportunities, on a daily basis, for mutual communication with your partner, even if it's only for fifteen minutes.

Spending time together and talking about the "stuff" going on in your head is critically important to a well-rounded, strong relationship. Unspoken thoughts influence the way communication unfolds in a relationship. How does your partner know what you are thinking or feeling if you never share it? Simply giving a look, shrugging your shoulders or rolling your eyes provides some information but falls short on many levels. Unless your partner is a mind reader, using only non-verbal communication will not be enough.

Take the next step and make it easier to be understood. Fill in the gaps so your partner can feel and understand your position. You may think they should know you well enough to interpret the non-verbal cues you are providing. Unfortunately, this assumption is a myth and will only keep your relationship from growing and reaching its full potential. You want to express what you are thinking and feeling in an open way that removes doubt. Isn't the goal to enhance communication rather than create a confusing puzzle that has to be solved?

When your viewpoint is clear your partner can better understand your perspective on the world. How can you have good communication if you are unclear about your loved one's perception? Asking questions and being curious is a good first step. Don't be shy or timid; ask for clarification of your partner's point of view if you are unclear. Ignoring the confusion will just create distance in your relationship.

I have found that couples may intentionally hold back what they share because they are concerned that their thoughts and emotions will have a negative impact on their relationship. By not clarifying your message you increase the likelihood of more problems down the road. A clear message with rich description will help your partner understand your position and allow for better communication. I often challenge couples to leave their comfort zone and begin to have a different kind of conversation than they usually have. A relationship will grow when you create space for it to be different than it was in the past. Shaking things up can be an effective way to explore novel and genuinely different experiences.

Think of your relationship as a living and changing organism. Relationships change over time. People change over time. The person you met many years ago is different than the person you're with now. Life experience changes everyone, and they will change your relationship. If your relationship does not adjust to these changes, there will be problems.

If you try to function the same way in year ten as in year one, you will notice problems. Getting clear about your partner's beliefs will help you have a better understanding of their perspective. Trying to guess what your partner means by what they are saying is an unnecessary risk. Why guess when you can simply ask?

All too often we make relationships more complex than they need to be. Answers are usually readily available if you ask. You are in the relationship together so why try to function as separate entities? If you only consider your own needs, you will lose your relationship. Of course, it can be quite frustrating when you are unable to find solutions. You may be inclined to ask others for their input. But heading down this road can be a dead-end. The answers are within your relationship. If you're having trouble finding them, seek out help so you can. One thing is certain, if you ignore your inability to communicate, things will get worse. Nothing improves on its own. Invest the time and your relationship will survive and thrive!

Some questions to consider:

- How would you know if your messages are unclear?

- What process do you engage in to bring greater clarity to your communication?

- Do you find any of your partner's messages confusing?

There's a reason that some of the most highly paid professionals in the world are absolute experts in effective communication. Clear, concise communication moves people to inspired action, compels them to want to be better at their work, their relationships, and their lives and motivates both individuals and groups to dare to do great and mighty things. At its most extreme, clear and effective communication saves lives and dramatically alters outcomes. Think hostage situations or critical negotiations.

Although maybe not quite as dramatic, don't underestimate the value or power of good communication. One excellent practice for how to communicate when you have a difficult message to convey is to ask yourself, if you were the one receiving this message, what would you want to hear and how would you want to hear it? Remember that what you say and how you say it are two different things and both are equally important. If you try to "hear" what you're going to say with the other person's ears, you might find that you want to communicate a bit differently.

**Relationship Exercise:**

Try to guess the TOP 5 messages YOU have shared with your partner that they may find confusing or unclear. Compare both of your lists and discuss useful ways to clarify your messages.

# SECRET #4

## Respect Changes

What you want from a relationship in the early months of dating may be quite different from what you want after you have been together for a while. Anticipate that both you and your partner will change over time. Feelings of love and passion change with time, as well.

Respecting and valuing these changes is healthy. Love literally changes brain chemistry for the first months of a relationship. For both physiological and emotional reasons, an established relationship can have a more complex and often richer level of passion than a new one.

In long-term relationships, the couple needs to make room for individual changes. All too often, couples want to monitor or limit how change should unfold. Controlling one another's behavior inhibits growth potential and results in emotional turmoil. Changing is part of life and part of all relationships. Attempts to shape someone's change will lead to resentfulness and bad feelings.

If you notice that your partner is changing in ways you find hard to accept then it is important to discuss your concerns. Ignoring what you are noticing will only make it worse. Ask your partner to explain the way he or she is seeing the world. Being able to walk in each other's shoes requires a sense of understanding and compassion. It's difficult to appreciate a change if you do not understand how that change makes sense to your loved one.

In most relationships, people don't say, "I am about to change (fill in the blank). Is that okay with you?" Why don't people ask this question? Probably because they are going to change their behavior regardless of whether it makes sense to you. Sometimes, too, change just happens without an intention behind it. As you move through life, your perspective changes. As you see the world differently, you adjust your behavior accordingly.

Change can take place within your awareness or outside your awareness. Often, if you ask your partner to change a particular behavior, they may think you are trying to control their actions. Showing interest and concern is different than attempting to manipulate your partner's behavior to match the perception or image in your mind.

Respecting changes requires that you appreciate your partner for the ways he or she is different than you. Too often people try to change the person they are with to meet their own expectations. Being able to embrace and respect changes in your partner shows that you genuinely care about them. Of course, we'd all love our partner to change in certain ways. However, trying to ensure this happens is a recipe for failure that will usually deteriorate the relationship over time.

In our **Relationship Coaching Program** at Relationships Unscripted, I encourage couples to provide space for changes in their relationship. Allowing one another to grow will nurture the relationship. A tree without sunlight and water will die. Your partner needs space to grow. Trying to monitor or control them will only suffocate your relationship and prohibit real growth over time. Respecting the ways your partner changes over the years is a way of communicating that you care. If you want someone to respect your changes, it's only fair for you to mirror that same behavior.

Changes are not always easy to see. While some changes are obvious, others may be just below the surface. If you notice changes that make you uncomfortable, or if you just want to understand them more, don't be afraid to initiate a conversation about it. Unless you're a mind-reader, you will most likely make a wrong guess. So try to ask questions and encourage your partner to share his or her perspective with you. Sometimes even your partner may not be aware of the changes that are occurring, especially when they happen over a long period of time. Slow changes take longer to see than abrupt changes, which are more obvious.

Spending time with one another will make you more familiar with your partner and help you notice even the most subtle changes. In today's world, everyone's lives are saturated with things to do and seemingly not enough time for the essential facets of our lives. The reality is that people usually find time for what they consider to be important. If your relationship is important to you, then take the time to learn about one another and stay connected. If not, the changes will appear as threats to the relationship rather than opportunities for growth.

Some questions to consider:

- What would be a sign that you are trying to influence how your partner changes?

- If you disagree with how your partner is changing, how can you respectfully approach them to express your concerns?

- Can you respect your partner's changes even if you do not fully agree with them?

Change is going to happen whether you want it to or not. Change can be exhilarating and exciting but it can also be scary and frustrating. In any relationship, when change happens for or to one person, it also happens to and for the other person. You may be excited about a certain change but be confused or irritated by your partner's lack of enthusiasm. Keep in mind that how each of you are going to experience the change is going to be different, and the overall effect of how the change ultimately shows up in the bigger picture will also probably be different. Be prepared to have conversations that may feel as if you and your partner aren't on the same emotional page. This can happen when the change is "good" as well as when the change is perceived as "bad" or at least not ideal.

You also want to be aware of the effects of change as it becomes the new normal. Enthusiasm may give way to discouragement or vice versa because it's hard to predict how change in the moment will look in the longer term. Staying attuned to how you and your partner are feeling will be important so you can continue to support each other.

**Relationship exercise:**

Sit down with your partner and discuss what changes each of you have made to enhance the relationship and which changes have created difficulties for you both. Ask one another which changes you would like to see continue and which you would like to go away. Share some insight with one another as to why the changes occurred and if they can be altered moving forward. Remember, changes happen in all relationship so respect your partner's answers and understand that acceptance is an important part of this exercise.

# SECRET #5

## Really Listen

Many books have been written on the subject of listening. Depending on the way you were raised, listening can mean many different things. Is it nodding your head with the "appearance" that you are agreeing or following the conversation? Is it the act of being quiet and not saying a word? Is listening saying, "You're right, honey" or "I agree with you?" Or can it be a few "uh huh" comments in response to what is being said?

Too often we create the illusion of listening because it is way too uncomfortable to listen to information that is boring, painful, unimportant, nonsensical, or just way too long. Ever watch a movie that you found to be boring or not entertaining? Were you really listening? Did you fake it? Probably so. Does "fake listening" work in a long-term relationship? As many of you already know, not very well. So the alternative is to learn how to LISTEN!

Listening does not mean you agree with what is being said. It is a way or connecting with your partner and showing that you care. Listening means you respect your partner. You can listen to a person and still maintain your own way of seeing the world. Supporting your partner and respecting his or her perspective helps to create a strong relationship.

It is not always easy to listen, especially after a long day of work, caring for the kids, not sleeping enough or experiencing other stresses. But excuses are not good reasons to ignore what your loved one is saying. Listening is an essential ingredient necessary for staying connected to your partner.

What are some of the key ingredients to good listening? Being a good listener requires the following: (a) don't interrupt, (b) focus on what your partner is saying rather than on formulating your own response, and (c) check out what you heard your partner say. You might start this process with: "I think you are saying..." or "What I understood you to say was..." This step alone can prevent misunderstandings that might otherwise develop into a fight.

Listening so that your partner feels listened to sends an incredibly powerful message. When you feel "heard," you feel validated. When you are listening to what your partner has to say, you are not responding or reacting. Listening means just that. If you are listening, you are not speaking! Listening does not mean you are agreeing or disagreeing. It shows you are open to accepting your partner's thoughts and feelings, without shooting him or her down or arguing. Couples who can accept each other's feelings are happier and feel safer and more secure.

### *Practice listening for the feelings behind the words, which is the true art of listening.*

As you become a more effective listener, your partner will feel freer to be more open and honest.

I often hear couples say "He/she is telling me one thing but means something else." An open and honest relationship requires that both people create enough space to listen to one another and be nonjudgmental. If you think that your partner won't care or be open to what you're saying, you're likely to feel inhibited in sharing the whole truth. Why share a heartfelt message with your partner if they are not really listening or couldn't care less about what you are saying? You're more apt to keep the information to yourself or find someone else to listen. The sad result is that your relationship will suffer and as a couple you'll grow further apart.

Learning effective listening takes time and patience. Yes, it is sometimes a slow process. At times, it can also unfold quickly if the couple becomes really good at listening. Isn't it easier to share openly with someone when you know he or she is listening? Or when you know your partner is supportive and willing to hear you out no matter how long it takes? Of course! Creating an environment that encourages listening will enhance your relationship and make it stronger in so many ways.

Some questions to consider:

- How do you know if your partner is really listening to you?

- Do you expect your partner to listen to you but fall short on listening to them?

- What changes can you make to show your partner you are a good listener?

- If you are unsure what your partner defines as good listening, can you ask them so you can have a better understanding?

When you really embrace listening, it can become one of life's most enjoyable and powerful endeavors! Really listening to what your partner is saying will give you incredible insight into what they are thinking and feeling *now* but it will also give you deeper insight into how they view the world. It's this filter, the way your partner sees and experiences life in general, that can create boundless opportunities to see the world as they see it and that will help you understand them and communicate with them better.

It's also important to be an *active* listener so that your loved one knows you really hear them. Nodding, murmuring, "Hmmm" or saying, "I understand" are great ways of active listening. Affirming what your partner is feeling and saying is also powerful. Saying things like, "I would have felt the same way" or "I can see why you are so upset" lets your partner know that you aren't judging them for what they are feeling and they have the right to their feelings. Be careful not to say too much though! A few words or one short sentence is okay but don't make the situation about you by affirming what their feeling and then launching into how you feel about the situation or explain your assessment of it. If you're truly listening, you are not doing much talking at all!

## Relationship Exercise:

Spend at least fifteen minutes listening to your partner without saying a word. Take turns with this exercise. After the exercise is completed, share what you "thought" he or she was saying. How accurate/inaccurate were you? Did you learn something new? How difficult was it to be patient and listen for the full fifteen minutes?  What if you practiced this exercise on a weekly basis?  How could it make a difference in your relationship?

# SECRET #6

## Nurture One Another and Show Compassion

Taking care of each other in special ways helps couples experience a warm, loving, intimate bond. When you were young, you engaged in nurturing behavior to show your love. Affection creates a connection that runs very deep. At the beginning of a relationship couples often engage in nurturing behavior to show love, support and an investment in the relationship. It feels good to nurture a loved one. It creates a deep emotional connection.

Nurturing can be expressed through simple behaviors such as a hug, smile or a slight touch. Verbally, it could be saying a few kind words like "everything is going to be okay" or "I'm sorry that you're having such a rough day." Nurturing shows you care! Nurturing is a necessary part of a growing, healthy relationship. It shows that you are invested in the relationship and want the best for each other.

In the **Relationship Coaching Program**, we discuss how nurturing behavior is very much connected to compassion. When you act in a compassionate way, you are telling your partner that you care about how he or she feels. No one wants to feel "alone" in a relationship. You want to feel like your partner is on life's journey with you. When you show compassion, you are telling your loved one that he or she is not alone. You are there to be supportive when things are going well as well as when life presents its challenges.

Compassion can be shown in many different ways. It could be the way you look at your partner or how attentively you listen. Sometimes, a little comment like, "I am here for you" can make all the difference. It is difficult to watch someone you care about go through struggles and challenging times. Consoling your partner and showing warmth will go a long way to creating a stronger relationship.

If you respond negatively to your partner when he or she is going through difficult times, you'll experience problems in your relationship. Ignoring your partner's emotionality will create an emotional disconnection in your relationship that could have negative repercussions moving forward. Sure, it's not always easy to listen to someone complaining or in pain. Maybe you had a long day at work or you are just not in the mood to listen and be compassionate.

Think about this: what if everyone only responded to their loved one's feelings or mood when they felt like it? What if you only showed compassion when you were feeling in the mood to be compassionate? Your partner will come to see you as self-centered and only caring about yourself. This kind of behavior will lead to arguments and deteriorate your relationship over time. So, the alternative is to suck it up and think about how you would want your partner to respond if you were feeling what they are feeling. Find that little extra ounce of energy to show you care. They'll appreciate it.

All relationships require sacrifices. Showing compassion is no different. Sometimes it is necessary to sacrifice at small moments in time for the betterment of the relationship. How many times have you said to yourself, "It feels so good to know my partner cares"? It's important to feel the person you are in a relationship with cares about you in a deep way. They are by your side to support you and encourage you. That's one of the benefits of being in a relationship rather than being by yourself.

Some questions you may want to consider:

- What do you believe nurturing behavior looks like?

- How can you let your partner know you like a particular behavior?

- What kinds of nurturing behaviors do you engage in?

- Does your partner realize when you are being nurturing?

- Are there some nurturing behaviors that you have stopped participating in? If so, why?

A relationship is a living thing and like all living things, will thrive with nurturing so don't overlook this important element. Take the time to find out what seems like nurturing to your partner so you are able to nurture them and their role in the relationship in a way that feels good to them. What you may feel is "nurturing" can feel like smothering or what you feel is smothering may just be the tip of nurturing for your partner. Different people need different levels of attention and you and your loved one need to determine and understand what that means for each of you.

As far as compassion, you can really never give too much. If you know the adage, "People won't remember much but they will always remember how you made them feel" then you understand the power of connectivity through compassion. When your partner feels heard, seen and understood, they will feel loved and when they feel loved, the relationship will continue to blossom.

Are you ready to explore what you MUST KNOW so your loved one will actually hear you and both people get what they want?

If you are getting sick and tired of staying stuck it's time to find out what you MUST DO consistently if you want to have passion, intimacy and great sex.

Isn't it time to uncover the essential ingredients to energize love and get back to that early dating, "giddy" feeling! (Yes, it's possible!). I invite you to stop by my website: http://relationshipsunscripted.com/programs/ to find out more about my monthly webinars and take the first step to re-igniting your relationship. I look forward to meeting you and helping you have the relationship you always desired!

**Relationship Exercise:**

Ask your partner and write down what he/she finds nurturing. Make a list of what you find nurturing. Share your responses and begin to create an idea of your partner's expectations in the relationship. Use these responses to include the identified behaviors into your daily lives. Remember, it is not necessary to do something big and extravagant to make your partner feel special and loved. One woman's list included a quick phone call from her partner during the day which made her feel he was thinking about her. Her partner asked her to cuddle with him at the end of the day while watching the evening news. Nurturing each other goes a long way.

Remember, love is a behavior not just words!

# SECRET #7

## If One of You Has a Problem,
## You Both Have a Problem

As a couple, it is essential that you focus on each other's needs. It is no longer just about you. Part of being in a relationship is having the ability to move beyond your limited perception. How does your partner perceive the situation? Often, something that you may not perceive to be a problem for you may be a problem for your significant other. You may be inclined to just "blow it off" because you are not experiencing any issues.

*If you ignore what your partner perceives as a problem you could end up having a bigger problem.*

This is why it makes sense to put yourself in your partner's shoes and to be aware of how they are feeling. How does your partner perceive an issue to be a problem? How is he or she being affected by the problem? How can you support your partner even though you are okay and don't necessarily feel there is a problem? Based on your partner's perception, they are struggling to move beyond or manage a situation that is negatively impacting their life. How can you be supportive or show empathy? Maybe, it's as simple as just listening and acknowledging them. Staying connected shows you care and you are there to help.

A simple rule to follow is:

### *If your partner has a problem, BOTH of you have problems.*

Why? Because the negative impact felt by one half of the couple will have an influence on both. Spend a day with your partner when he or she is having a problem and notice the effect it has on you. Try to stay in a good mood when your partner has a problem and see what happens. Attempt to ignore your partner's problem and act like everything is okay. How do things unfold? Not very well. Your partner's emotions will have an effect on you, and if you see your partner's problem as theirs alone and not yours, you'll soon experience increased tension. Your partner will perceive you as not caring or being emotionally detached. It's never beneficial to have your partner feel alone with their problem while you have removed yourself from the equation.

### *One way of staying emotionally connected is to own the problem together.*

An important side note: sharing the problem does not mean you are bothered by the problem as much as your partner. It's just that you are showing compassion and the willingness to be there for your partner. It's easier to manage a problem if you know your partner is by your side and is fully supportive. It makes little difference if the issue is a concern for you or not. It's simply about moving beyond your personal perception and letting your partner know that you are "all in." You and your partner are on the same team. The only way a team works well together is if everyone takes ownership of the team. When one person is injured, the others step up and help. When the chips are down everyone pitches in. Isn't it great to know that you are never alone? That's why you choose to share your life with someone; because you are literally sharing your problems, challenges, hopes, dreams, pain, sadness, joy and amazing breakthroughs. You share it all!

Some questions to consider:

- How do you let your partner know that they are not alone when experiencing a problem?

- How do you support them when he or she is experiencing a problem?

- Is there some advice you can give your partner about how to support you when you are trying to manage a problem?

Something to really consider when you aren't necessarily the one with the "problem," is to remember that patience and those good listening skills and compassion you just read about will come in very handy at this point! Getting irritated because your partner won't move as quickly through the problem as you would like won't solve anything and will probably cause a breakdown in communication. Practice patience in helping your loved one move through the problem and let them know that you're in this together.

Also be careful not to "solve" the problem because it can send the message that the feelings behind it aren't valid and that everything will be okay once your partner has the "answer". Problems are often a process that by their very nature, are meant for growth purposes so don't be in a hurry to move your loved one through the problem too quickly because you're tired of hearing about it. Instead, ask good questions and create opportunities to have good conversations around what is going on so that you move through the situation together.

## Relationship Exercise:

Ask your partner how you can show support for them when they are coping with a problem. Give each other some pointers and insight as to how you can feel more emotionally connected when experiencing a problem. Share with one another new things you've learned from this exercise. Then, jump right in and start to practice these new insights in your relationship.

# SECRET #8

## Accept Conflict as Part of Any Intimate Relationship

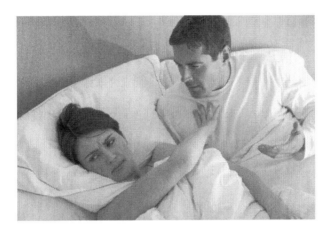

Do happily married couples argue with one another? They sure do. Conflict is a natural part of all relationships. Think of it as an opportunity to learn about the way(s) your partner is seeing his or her world. Conflicts in a relationship are inevitable. It is important to understand that it serves many purposes. Conflict helps us to become aware of problems that need to be resolved. When your partner is upset about something they are clueing you into his or her world. Listen to the struggles and challenges that are being shared. Through talking about the problem your partner will feel closer to you and your relationship will grow closer. Don't you want your partner to be able to turn to you rather than outside sources? If your partner does not feel comfortable approaching you, they'll find other people outside your relationship to share their problems with. This is a recipe for more problems. Creating a safe environment in which your partner knows that conflict can be discussed is an important ingredient to a thriving relationship.

Conflict helps reduce the day-to-day annoyances that occur when relating to another person. Through conflict we learn about what works and what does not work in our relationships. Use these experiences as opportunities to gauge how your relationship is progressing and what needs to be addressed.

If your partner is openly sharing their problems it's a good indication they feel comfortable being authentic with you. You want your partner to share his or her challenges and struggles. A closer relationship is built on understanding differences. Only then can you begin to create new paths and bridges that keep you connected. Keeping the information to yourself leads to more problems down the road.

In my work with couples, I often get asked, "How much do I share with (my significant other)?" This is a great question. The answer is probably different for each person based on his or her comfort level and openness in the relationship. An easy answer is that it depends on how much you want your partner to know about you. How vulnerable do you want to make yourself? Remember, the less you share, the less risk you take. The more you share the greater risk you take. However, your decision should not be purely based on risk. In a long-term relationship, if you take no risks to become vulnerable and instead keep yourself safe, you will never reap the rewards of a fulfilling and emotionally connected relationship. So, no risk -- few rewards.

Will your relationship suffer if you keep most everything to yourself? The answer is YES. How can you nurture a relationship when you do not discuss conflict and you keep important feelings and beliefs to yourself? You are kidding yourself if you think you can play it safe and still have an emotionally deep and fulfilling relationship. So, you are always left with a choice. Step into conflict and build skills to overcome challenges or pretend everything is okay and let the problems increase over time until you eventually no longer have a relationship.

### *Ignoring conflict creates an emotional distance in your relationship.*

It may be important to remind yourself that addressing the conflict will make your relationship stronger. Love is not just based on the "good stuff." It's also deeply rooted in knowing that you will work with one another to overcome challenges. In fact, your emotional bond will grow stronger as you learn to manage conflict as a couple.

One of the greatest challenges in overcoming conflict is attempting to avoid more of the same wrong solution. If the solution that you are attempting to put in place is not resolving the issue, move on to another option. It's often easy to think that you should keep on trying the same solution because it makes sense. What may make sense to you may not make sense for the relationship. Consequently, the solution becomes the problem in some instances. By letting go of the solution, you increase the possibility of new information entering into your relationship.

Letting go of your ego can be the first step in resolving a problem in a relationship. Your ego is what tells you to keep trying the same solution because you do not want to admit that what you were doing was not working. When you let go of your ego, you free up your mind to think in new and different ways. This can be quite helpful in discovering new perspectives and solutions that could resolve the conflicts in the relationship.

Another part of managing conflict is examining your conflict management style. Is it working? If not, you may want to consider experimenting with other styles. In a successful relationship there are many conflicts, but they are managed with respect. Understanding how your partner manages conflict is an important part of preserving respect. Everyone handles conflict differently and respecting these differences will allow your relationship to resolve problems.

When couples begin to address differences in a relationship, there is often a struggle over who is right and wrong. Unfortunately, proving you are right and your partner is wrong will not solve any conflicts. It may make you feel better but will not help your relationship move to a better place regarding finding resolutions. Letting go of the right and wrong concept increases the likelihood that you will more productively let go of long-standing differences.

Over a long-term relationship, couples often stockpile problems and resentment. It's much more effective to deal with the problems immediately using clear and specific language. Keep your cool and describe the issue as you see it. Don't make generalizations and avoid sweeping statements. That only keeps the conflict stuck in neutral with little hope of altering its course moving forward.

In addition, be careful what you say during the conflict. Once words are spoken, they are released into the world. The impact could be alarming, changing the direction of the conflict and even the direction of the relationship. Words can cut like a knife and create harm for the couple moving forward. Preserving respect will ensure that words are use cautiously and with great thought.

When I work with couples, some of the problems most difficult to overcome involve words spoken in anger that affect the relationship deeply. Those words are played back again and again. The resulting pain becomes deeper and the wound takes longer to heal. Sometimes these wounds will create scars that never go away. They may be hidden but often create a roadblock for a relationship as the couple attempts to move forward. So be careful what you say and how you say it. When words fly out of your mouth, they are gone and the repercussions can last a lifetime!

Some questions to consider:

- Do you know how to manage conflict in your relationship without escalating the issues?

- Are you able to discuss differences while still maintaining respect?

- Do you know when you have "crossed the line?"

- Should that happen, do you know how to re-establish communication with your partner?

When you find yourself in a conflict, pay particular attention to what is *not* being said as well as what *is* being said. Body language or a change in behavior is very revealing so try to stay extra alert and aware to what is going on during this time. Again, just as when you find yourself with a problem, don't try to hurry the situation to its end. Profound and powerful changes can occur in the midst of conflict so give your partner the space they need to work through things in the manner they prefer. Be sensitive to the personality of your partner too. Don't try to get an extravert to process thing internally and don't try to get an introvert to talk about how they are feeling until they are ready. It may also be a good idea to gently state what you need (more time, more space, etc.) to your partner, since in the midst of a conflict, it may not be clear.

Above all, remember that conflict is normal and it doesn't mean you have a bad relationship or that you're breaking up. Take a deep breath and look at the ways conflict can strengthen your relationship.

### Relationship Exercise:

The first goal in this exercise is to stay clear of having a conflict as you talk about conflict. Once this understanding is established, the next step is for both of you to write your "TOP 10" areas of conflict in your relationship. Write this list together. After the list is completed, brainstorm together how you can address the conflicts in a productive way moving forward. What insights and solutions did you uncover?

# SECRET #9

## Check-in Periodically

An important part of staying connected in a relationship is finding time to check-in with your significant other. Touching base with one another allows you to stay connected and show support. In today's rapidly moving world, if you do not keep up with the changes each of you are experiencing, you may start growing apart.

When you check-in with your partner, you are increasing each other's awareness in the relationship. The conversations that follow will create greater understanding of your differences. On a weekly basis, schedule time to see how your significant other is doing. Small check-ins can also occur during the workday. For example, you can schedule a time to talk during lunch hour or on the way home. There's no specific measure for how often you should check-in with your partner. It really depends on what the couple agrees to. In some relationships, partners may talk in the morning, lunchtime and in the evening.  In other relationships, the couple may text ten times a day.  Although there is no standard amount of time to touch base, once or twice a day should be the bare minimum.

Part of the check-in process involves setting time aside to talk about your relationship. What's going well?  What needs improvement?   Communicating about expectations and goals should be part of this process. If there is something that has been lingering or bothering you, let your significant other hear about it. Sharing the positive experiences in your life is also valuable.

If you want your relationship to improve, let your partner know the things they're doing or saying that you enjoy. Don't be shy about sharing the challenges you are experiencing or areas of communication that you find confusing.  Avoiding or ignoring difficult topics for too long can result in the relationship drifting into rocky waters without either of you even noticing. Sometimes there are lingering concerns that are ignored. No one likes conflict because it makes things uncomfortable.

***The more normal you make checking in as a part of your relationship, the easier it will be to talk about any issues that may need to be addressed.***

In our **Relationship Coaching Program**, a common pitfall for couples is attempting to guess what one another is thinking. This guessing process occurs both within and outside of the therapy sessions. After spending several years in a relationship, it can be quite easy to assume that your partner should know what you are thinking. But is it fair to expect them to be a mind reader? Of course not! You may assume that he or she should know you well enough so you don't have to explain everything. However, knowing someone does not mean you always know their thoughts. Thoughts are influenced by emotions. As emotions change so do thoughts. So, a person in a good mood will think and communicate very differently than someone in a bad mood.

When you check-in with your partner, try to get a sense of his or her emotional state. Consider how the person is feeling as you begin to communicate. How your partner hears and understands what you are saying is very much connected to their emotional state. Emotions influence how your partner is thinking and perceiving the world. An important way to show respect for your partner is to acknowledge his or her emotions.

As you do your check-in together, ask questions rather than assuming your partner already knows what you are thinking. How many times have you tried to guess their thoughts and were wrong? It's probably over 50% of the time for most couples. If you make an assumption, never check-in to see if it's accurate, and then engage in behavior based on that assumption, things will usually not turn out well. As you move ahead based on this faulty assumption, you may wonder, "Why is he/she being so difficult?" Guess what? You guessed wrong! Now, you are confused about why you've entered troubled waters.

***When you believe something is true in your relationship and never confirm your belief, you take a big risk!***

No matter how well you know your partner, it's always wise to ask, "Here's what I think. Are we on the same page?" Once you have this information – confirmed – then you can move forward. Otherwise you are just guessing and hoping you are right.

When you check-in throughout the week with your partner, remember that life gets busy so you may have to schedule a specific time to touch base. If your daytime is very crowded, wait until the evening. The best check-ins are the ones that occur face to face. When you can see body language and nonverbal responses to what you are saying, you will have a better indication of your loved one's position.

It is a good idea to take turns talking as you check-in with one another. Everyone wants to be heard. So sometimes you may want to rush in and let it out. Listening is just as much a part of checking in as talking. Being quiet when your partner is talking allows you to listen better and gives each of you a chance to be heard as you take turns. When your partner is done, you may want to ask questions or just show support. You can also ask how you can be the most helpful in supporting them and their needs.

When check-ins lead to "positive vibes" you increase the likelihood of touching base more often and you will stay more connected. If you or your partner thinks the check-ins are a waste of time, they will happen less often. You need to create a safe, compassionate and supportive environment so check-ins will lead to meaningful opportunities to nurture your relationship.

You will often find when the relationship is going well you may check-in more often and when the relationship is deteriorating check-ins will be less frequent. Ideally, check-ins should take place more often when the relationship is not going well because you need to find more opportunities to connect with one another. Often the last thing you want to do is talk to your partner when you think it will lead to an argument. As a result, you do not check-in and try to talk as little as possible. Over time, this decision will lead to a deterioration of the relationship.

A better strategy at those times is to step it up and step into the uncomfortable conversation and check-in. Meeting the discomfort head-on will strengthen your couple skills into overcoming roadblocks. Pressing through the discomfort will take your relationship to new heights.

***Your ultimate goal is to be "checking in" rather than "checking out" of your relationship.***

Establishing this connection when the relationship may not be going well will build some strength and resiliency into your relationship. It will also be a reminder for both of you that your relationship is strong enough to withstand challenging times. The effort to check-in will be worth it and will keep your relationship heading in the right direction!

Some questions to consider:

- How often do you check-in on a weekly basis in your relationship?

- When was the last time you talked with your partner about "important" issues?

- Do you sometimes touch base with your partner and intentionally talk about "easy stuff" rather than issues that may be impacting your relationship?

- Has staying away from the difficult issues created more problems? If so, what skills can you put in place to help you address the "difficult stuff"?

Checking in might take some getting used to, especially if once a day to you borders on overkill and for your partner, it's just the beginning. Regardless of where you fall on the scale, when you make an effort to connect over the little things, connecting over the bigger things will seem easier.

Establishing a ritual of checking in will help you create verbal intimacy, which will help create other kinds of intimacy. Women in particular, like to know that their partner is thinking of them throughout the day and a simple phone call or text can go a long way to establishing a sense of intimacy that will last well into the evening!

### Relationship Exercise:

It's time to play a fun "guessing game." Sit down with your partner and ask how often he/she believes you should check-in over a period of a week. What are your expectations? What are your partner's expectations? Ask your partner how you could be supportive during the check-ins. Find out what has been working well and not so well during past check-ins. Begin to explore new ways of checking in that will work for the relationship.

*Dr. Jeff Kane*

# SECRET #10

## Accept Differences and Respect Your Partner's Rights.

It is difficult, but healthy, to accept that there are some things about our partners that will not change over time, no matter how much we want them to. When you are in love with someone and see behavior that you would like changed, it's important to remember that it is ultimately up to your partner whether or not that change will happen.

Your partner may change temporarily just to keep you happy or stop you from bothering him or her. But this type of change is temporary. Long-term change only takes place when someone desires to change and has committed to doing the work that is necessary to make that change. Doing

63

all of that also requires that is makes sense to them and they understand that the rewards of change are going to be worth it. If it does not make sense, they will eventually return to the original behavior. Trying to force a change in your partner will ultimately be a waste of time. In addition, it will lead to more arguments and create an emotional disconnection in the relationship.

One way of making sure your relationship will not last is by creating an environment in which both partners tell one another how to act. That creates two people trying to control each other. The only behavior you should control is your own. Being pushy with your partner and imposing your view will lead to arguments and resentfulness. A better option is to accept differences and move on.

In our coaching program, I have routinely found that some couples have beliefs that keep them from inviting change into their lives. You may hold the belief or unrealistic expectation that your partner will never change from the way he or she is now. Your partner is capable of change. You are capable of change as well. Being capable of changing and initiating change are two different things. A person has to first identify something wrong that needs to be changed. Then, they have to desire to make the changes. This evolution usually comes from self-examination and requires some insight. Life experiences can sometimes help the process along.

***Remember, it's ultimately up to your partner to change;
it is not up to you to change your partner.***

In the end, accepting your differences may lead to change or may result in respecting different perspectives.

In healthy relationships, there is respect for each partner's right to have her/his own feelings, friends, activities and opinions. It is unrealistic to expect or demand that your partner have the same priorities, goals, and interests as you. Respect does not mean that you agree with your partner's opinion or perspective. It means you create space in your relationship for each other to have an opinion. It's okay to see the same picture differently. It's vitally important to create room so you and your partner's views can be heard and understood.

***Validation of one another's perspective is part of
respecting one another.***

When you listen rather than judge your partner's behavior, you are showing respect. Honoring your partner means that you honor his or her view even if you see things differently. Each person moves through the world marching to the beat of a different drum. Your partner may like different music or food than you. In a relationship, you bring your culture and experiences with you. Many of these differences will not fade away no matter how much you love one another. Accepting these differences will lead to mutual respect. Appreciating the differences will result in a closer relationship. No one ever said being in a relationship was always going to be a cake walk. It takes patience and a willingness to play nicely and respectfully.

Many of the rules created around respect are put in place early in a relationship. Respecting your partner's right to see the world in his or her own way is critically important. Although most people do not think of "rights" when they think about relationships, it is part of maintaining respect for one another.

When you feel respected, you are more likely to share openly and freely. You are not worried about being judged. When your rights are not respected, you may feel compelled to act or behave in a way that is different from who you are just to keep things going well. Have you ever felt like you were putting on a façade in your relationship? In other words, you were behaving differently than how you felt just to stay away from arguments. This is playing a role that is not really you, also known as "faking it." If you begin to fake it long enough, your partner will begin to believe that's how you really are.

Be careful of the patterns you create. Once they are put in place, they are very difficult to change. Being your "raw" and "real" self is essential in a relationship. No hiding, faking or pretending. Showing the natural and authentic you should be enough. If it's not, the relationship is going to fail.

Some questions to consider:

- Do you find it difficult to respect your partner's view if you see the same issue from a different perspective?

- Can you disagree with your partner without harboring ill will or bad feelings?

- Are there some differences that you find difficult to accept?

One of the most important things to understand about differences is that you can't change one aspect of someone's character traits without it showing up in every other way in their life and you might find you don't much care for that!

For example, say your partner is more of an introvert and fairly sensitive. These qualities usually show up in that your partner is a good care-taker and in fact, takes good care of *you*. Nurturing and being demonstratively affectionate are usually common for someone with these types of traits and they are probably also intuitive, which means they can sense what you need, often before you do.

Now, let's say you have moments where you wish your partner were more entertaining or interesting at social gatherings or that sometimes you wish they would have a thicker skin. Sure, that sounds appealing and in certain situations, it would be great. However, the very things that make your loved one so great at taking care of you and intuitively sensing what you need wouldn't exist if they were more of an extravert and not sensitive. The two sets of traits are incongruent. Everyone's best traits are usually their worst; it all depends on context.

So, the next time you find yourself not appreciating the different way your partner sees the world, shows up in the world and interacts in the world, think of all the ways that those exact things are what you probably love most about them!

> Does your relationship feel like "groundhog day?" You know, the same old problems day after day! It's FRUSTRATING when you want to work things out but feel too exhausted to try and have the relationship you want. Isn't it time to change it to something better?" The secret to solving any problem is getting ANSWERS that really work. Are you ready to explore the relationship mistakes that get in the way of your happiness? You are invited to attend my monthly complimentary webinars. I invite you to stop by http://relationshipsunscripted.com/programs/ to find out more and take the first step to re-igniting your relationship. I look forward to meeting you and helping you have the relationship you always desired!

## Relationship Exercise:

Sit down with your partner and make a list of the ways you are different. The list may be short or long. The size of the list does not really matter. After your lists have been completed, create another list of the ways you are the same. What did you find out? Don't get too nervous if your list of differences is greater than your list of similarities. Begin to look at how you can begin to respect these differences in your relationship. Acceptance is the first step to moving closer to one another.

*Dr. Jeff Kane*

# SECRET #11

## Maintaining the Relationship
## While Remaining Honest and Trustworthy

Most of us know that keeping a vehicle moving well in the right direction takes more than just regular refueling. It also requires ongoing maintenance and active corrections to the steering to compensate for changes in the road. It's much the same for ongoing healthy relationships. While we may work hard to get the relationship started, expecting to cruise without effort or active maintenance usually leads the relationship to stall or crash!

Maintaining a relationship takes work, time, and an investment. If you do the little things to keep the relationship going well, you will find that the maintenance requires less energy. A well-maintained relationship takes less energy than a relationship that is not maintained. For example, if you provide your car with regular tune-ups, there will be fewer breakdowns and repairs required over the lifetime of the car. Sometimes we wait until our relationship is in disarray before we attempt to intervene. Maintenance requires that you check with your partner regularly and share openly about each other's discomfort.

Though gifts and getaways are important, it is often the small, nonmaterial things that partners routinely do for each other that keep the relationship satisfying. As discussed earlier, listening, checking in, nurturing, apologizing, giving emotional support and respecting changes are all part of maintaining a relationship.

The amount of maintenance required will depend on many factors.

- How much alike or different are you?

- How strong is your emotional bond?

- Do you have clear and consistent communication?

- Do you respect one another's right to see the world differently?

- Do you show one another affection on a regular basis?

The more connected you are in these areas, the more likely your relationship will require less maintenance. If you are doing the small things along the way, there is less chance of a breakdown looming ahead. Investing in your relationship over time has big payoffs down the road.

One of the core values necessary for a fulfilling relationship is honesty. Without honesty in place, you no longer have a relationship. Honesty can sometimes make things uncomfortable in a relationship. You may hear something you wished you had never heard. You may share a thought that may hurt your partner's feelings.

***Sharing in an honest manner starts with digging deep down into your soul and being honest with yourself.***

How do you think and feel about your world? How do you describe these thoughts and feelings to your partner with respect? Talking in an honest way does not mean being abrasive or rude. Some people are more direct than others. Before opening up to your partner, ask yourself,

***"What is the best way I can share this information in a compassionate and thoughtful manner?"***

73

When I work with couples in the coaching program, I challenge them to evaluate how they approach difficult issues. We explore the power of words and the impact they have on their relationship. Once words are said, they are gone. You are unable to take them back. So, it makes sense to take some time and make sure you have reviewed your position before sharing your reality with your partner. There are always softer, kinder and gentler ways to express your honesty. It may take a little time for you to review your thoughts before sharing them. The time you spend deciding what you want to say will save you much time that would be spent on arguing down the road.

Be aware that honesty can still make things uncomfortable in your relationship. When you talk in an honest way, invite your partner into a conversation about the information you have shared. Be sure to listen and resist becoming defensive. Your honesty will promote honesty in return. You can expect to hear some things you wished you had never heard. Although it may be uncomfortable to hear the words leave your partner's mouth, it is important to let them lead to real and meaningful communication. The relationship can be stronger in the long run.

As you begin to create a strong, fulfilling relationship based on honesty, you will also be building a more trusting relationship. One of the fastest ways for a relationship to deteriorate is to question your partner's trustworthiness. Trust is born out of knowing your partner in a deep way over time. Trust is built from a foundation of consistency and being true to one's word. There is a connection between what you say and what you do. Your words and actions must match one another. Empty promises will diminish trust in a relationship. Be true to what you say and make sure you follow through.

You may be tempted to try and "fake" (a.k.a. lying) being honest because you are concerned about the repercussions from talking openly with your partner. This approach may work for a while, but over time these illusions of trust will wither away and life will reveal the fallacies that have been created. Once trust is questioned or violated, your relationship will be changed in a permanent way. The scars can run deep. Have you ever had a surgical procedure on your body? How long after you were "healed" did you realize that you would never be the same? Once certain lines in a relationship have been crossed, your relationship is changed forever. This doesn't mean your relationship will not thrive again. People heal from injuries (physical and emotional) all the time. Re-establishing trust, however, is a long road. The steps necessary to regain trust is beyond the scope of this book. Suffice it to say, it's much easier maintaining trust than trying to regain it once it's been lost.

Some questions to consider:

- How often do you engage in behaviors to maintain the stability of your relationship?

- What steps do you take to insure that your relationship is being maintained in a healthy direction?

- How do you know you can trust your partner?

- If you were honest with your partner 100% of the time, would your relationship change? If so, in what way(s)?

The best way to ensure that you maintain honesty with your partner is to be certain that you are always being honest with yourself. It's going to be difficult to share your feelings honestly with your loved one when you are in denial with yourself about how you are actually feeling.

Practice creating extreme honesty with yourself at all times so you become aware when you are not sharing openly and honestly with your partner. Stuffing your feelings so that you convince yourself you are feeling "fine" and then saying that to your loved one is a great disservice to you both. A relationship cannot become all that it's meant to become if one or both of you have gotten good at not being honest with yourselves. Challenge each other to be honest, to be raw and real internally as well as externally. Let your partner know that you are strong enough to take their honesty and that you won't punish them for having feelings or perceptions that are different from yours.

**Relationship Exercise:**

Create a list of the activities you engage in that maintain your relationship. Take turns reviewing each other's lists. You can add to one another's lists and give each other advice on how both lists even better. Remember to be honest when writing your list.

# SECRET #12

## Intimacy

Many couples believe intimacy is an act that happens in one specific place. Want to guess where this place is? Yes, in the bedroom. Intimacy may lead you to the bedroom, but it starts way before you jump into bed.

Intimacy is the smile or hug that you give one another in the morning before going to work. Intimacy is the peck on the cheek after your partner cooks a great meal. Intimacy is the little way you flirt with your partner around your home or the text message you send while you are away from one another. Intimacy is the little card or flower that shows you care. Intimacy is the kind and gentle words you use when talking to each other. Intimacy is the raising of the eyebrows or subtle expressions that show you find your partner "hot." Intimacy is the wink or smile you give when you see your partner leave the shower. Intimacy could be a long hug or flirting. Intimacy might be coming home a little earlier and letting your partner know that he or she is missed. Of course, the list goes on and on.

If you take care of these little things outside the bedroom, you will increase the likelihood of enjoying what happens when you're in the bedroom. There are several differences in the way men and women perceive intimacy; that's a separate book in itself. In general, woman like compassion, warmth, closeness and all the other little things that make them feel special. For men, it's often about the "let's get down to business" mentality. Some of these areas overlap as do many of the characteristics of each gender since not all men or all women think and act alike. The key is to respect and understand the expectations of your partner. Each relationship is different and unique in its own way.

Without intimacy in a relationship, couples struggle to be happy. Intimacy creates sparks that keeps a relationship strong and thriving. Think of intimacy as a way of being rather than a switch that is either on or off. If you act in an intimate way with your partner, you will feel closer and more connected. Intimacy keeps things exciting and vibrant.

Since every relationship is a little different, intimacy is a little different for every couple. What may turn one person on may disgust someone else. What you may think is sexy your partner might find raunchy. Don't assume if you think a particular behavior is wonderful that your loved one will agree with you.

In our **Relationship Coaching Program**, I explain that one of the keys to fulfilling intimacy is to serve your partner rather than serve yourself. If you serve your partner well, your plate should never be empty. Acting in a self-serving way will not enhance your relationship. Everyone has needs. Part of respecting one another is finding a way to understand and communicate your needs to your partner. Intimacy may not unfold in the exact way you want it. There has to be some give and take. It's not about "me;" it's all about "we."

Think of intimacy as oxygen for your relationship. If you keep intimacy alive, your relationship will thrive. Without intimacy you have removed the oxygen from the relationship and you can only survive so long. You can place your relationship on life support but eventually, if you fail to engage in the behavior necessary to preserve intimacy, the plug will be pulled. Either you or your partner will begin to become emotionally detached without the oxygen that intimacy provides.

Once you begin to regularly practice intimacy, it will become an integral part of your relationship. At first, it may seem like a lot of work. Like any new activity, in the beginning it will require more energy until it becomes part of your daily routine, just like when you first started going to the gym, or began any other commitment. You may have said to yourself, "I am not in the mood; this is too much work," but as you continue to push yourself week after week, month after month, you begin to realize the benefits. One day, you see there is a payoff for your efforts. You feel better and more energized. You're thinking clearer and can concentrate better. You may feel less stress. Before you know it, the gym has become part of your weekly routine.

The same philosophy holds true for intimacy. Once intimacy becomes a "way of being" with your partner, the benefits will be so rewarding that you will not want to stop being intimate. Soon, acting in an intimate way will feel natural and you will forget you are doing it. It will just be that way. Intimacy will be a natural extension of you. You and your relationship will benefit.

Some questions to consider:

- How do you show intimacy to your partner in your relationship?

- Are there times when you are unclear about the intimacy intentions of your partner?

- Do you and your partner have a different idea of what intimacy looks like in your relationship?

- If so, have you talked about these differences?

There are many different kinds of intimacy and life is richer when you experience them all, especially with your partner! Be open to learning, understanding and embracing what is "intimate" to your loved one. There is nothing more rewarding than creating special moments, memories and ultimately, magic with the person you love and who loves you.

## Relationship Exercise:

Make a list of what forms of intimacy you feel you are missing in your relationship. Try to guess what kinds of intimacy your partner would like more of. Share this list with one another and compare your similarities and differences. Be playful and begin to pick a few behaviors from each other's list for the upcoming week. See what you find out. Remember, intimacy will begin to shift in your relationship as you begin to think of intimacy as a way of being not an act that only happens when you enter your bedroom.

As a side note....

I will be releasing a new, exciting, life-changing program that will alter the way couples understand their relationships. During my twenty years of working with couples, I have uncovered some organic ingredients and fundamental tools that I have used with my clients to help them create and maintain SPARX in their relationships. I am excited about sharing these insights with you and seeing how these ingredients can change the nature of your relationship.

So, if you are ready to wake up your sleepy relationship, jump on board and let's take a ride together. There are lots of insights, surprises and "a-ha" moments around the corner. So, put your seatbelt on and take this journey into a new world of understanding relationships. It's all about the SPARX – keeping things fresh, alive and exciting!

**Some concluding thoughts ...**

The 12 "Secrets" I've shared with you are a great starting point to begin making changes in your relationship. The ideas are generalized for the purposes of talking about most relationships. Please understand that every relationship is different. Your relationship is unique in its own way and not all of the ideas or exercises described will fit all relationships. This book is not a replacement for couples therapy or another type of therapeutic intervention. The information can be used as a general guide and as an opportunity to uncover some underlying concerns in your relationship.

After reading through this book, I encourage you to sit down with your partner and go through some of the exercises. Communicate about what you have discovered. Be open to the opportunity of changing your relationship. Just because you have done things the same way for years does not mean that you have to continue the same way moving forward. If you open yourself to change, change will enter your life. An open heart and an open mind are the beginning requirements. From there, anything is possible.

If the solutions you have attempted to use have not resolved your problems, reach out to friends, family, loved ones, or a professional. Sometimes you may be unable to find the answers on our own. Admitting that you are unable to resolve problems on your own is an important realization. It's a known fact that when you are too close to a problem you are often unable to find the perspective you need and the solutions you so desperately want. Never give up on reaching your goals as a couple. Relationships are not a sprint; they are a marathon!

If you're **tired of having a relationship that isn't fulfilling** and are ready to put the spark and sizzle back into it, visit Dr. Jeff Kane at http://relationshipsunscripted.com/relationshipassessmentsession to fill out an assessment and see if you qualify for a complimentary consultation ($297 value).

---

**RECEIVE YOUR FREE COPY TODAY!**

***SECRETS TO STAYING MARRIED FOR 50 YEARS***

***(OR MORE!)***

During the 20 years I've worked with couples, I have found there are some common ingredients of long-term relationships. I invite you to stop by http://relationshipsunscripted.com/staymarriedover50years to receive your **FREE COPY** of the "secrets" to a long lasting, fulfilling marriage.

---

## About the Author

Dr. Jeff Kane is the Founder of Family Therapy Center, a private practice with two locations in South Florida. He is also the Founder and CEO of Relationships Unscripted, a global community for couples to grow their relationship and keep their "spark" alive. Since 1994, Dr. Kane has demonstrated his passion for helping couples create shifts in their relationships so they can experience greater happiness. Dr. Kane helps his clients find the underlying causes of their issues and guides them in creating the kind of relationships they truly desire. Dr. Kane is dedicated to teaching his clients how to strengthen their relationships through better communication, patience, kindness and understanding of one another. He credits his nineteen year marriage and strong family bond with his wife and their eleven and sixteen year-old sons to the principles he not only teaches others but lives himself.

Dr. Kane provides relationship coaching and strategy sessions with couples around the world in his online community RelationshipsUnscripted.com.

The **Relationship Coaching Program** can be enjoyed via Skype or telephone. RelationshipsUnscripted.com offers complimentary webinars each month and programs that you can enjoy from the comfort of your home. Also, you can visit Dr. Jeff Kane on the inspirational page he started with his wife, Sherry, at Facebook.com/RelationshipsUnscripted.

If you have questions about relationship coaching sessions, online courses or programs, products or services you can send your request to: info@RelationshipsUnscripted.com or call 1-844-MORE-LUV.

**Media Contacts:**

Print Media and Article Publishing:
media@relationshipsunscripted.com

TV and Radio Interviews:
media@relationshipsunscripted.com

Provide a review of this book on Amazon and receive a FREE copy of Dr. Kane's guide to *"9 Powerful Ways to Show Love in Your Relationship"*. After providing the review, send an email with the words "BOOK REVIEWED" in the subject line to info@RelationshipsUnscripted.com and the free copy will be sent.